PASSIVE INCOME IDEAS IN THE 21st CENTURY

Author: Ken Horton

Contents

Chapter 1 5

Types of Passive Income 7

What Amount Would You Be Able to Earn from Passive Income? 7

Self-Charged Interest 9

Investment Properties 9

What Is Passive Real Estate Investing? 13

What Is Residual Income? 15

How Can You Generate Additional Residual Income? 15

4 Reasons Passive Income Investing Might Be for You 17

You Won't Have to Deal with Toilets, Tenants, or Trash 17

You Won't Have to Deal with a Bank 18

Your Passive Investment Lets You Leverage the Expertise and Experience of Others 18

You Can Make Money While You Sleep 19

Chapter 2 20

Designing and Selling T-Shirts Online Can Be Amazing and Profitable. 22

Merch by Amazon 25

Chapter 3 27

Passive income through advertising a car 27

Chapter 4 29

Affiliate Marketing 29

Chapter 5 31

Sell Digital Files on Etsy 31

Chapter 6 33

Rent out your car 33

Chapter 7 35

Udemy 35

Chapter 8 37

Create an app 37

Chapter 9 39

Create a blog or YouTube channel..39

Chapter 10 42

Rent out different items..42

Chapter 11 45

Sell Stock Photos 45

Chapter 12 47

Become a Drop-shipper 47

Chapter 13 49

Refinancing your mortgage...49

Chapter 14 52

Car Wash 52

Chapter 15 54

Peer-to-peer income 54

Conclusion 56

Chapter 1

When we earn **money** with a paid job, this process is known as 'active income.' On the other hand, 'passive income' is a way of making money without having to work for it every day. Most passive **income** ideas require some work or investment initially, but if you're successful you can continue earning an immense amount of money over time.

Some of the most popular passive income streams include royalties, rental income, investments, and affiliate marketing. Passive income is more appealing because it requires less work and offers unlimited earning opportunities. It can take some time to make enough money to live on and the market is becoming more competitive. You can create a blog or an app to make passive income. All you must do is set aside some time and money. If you are smart, you could make a lot of money while you sleep.

There are three main types of income: dynamic income, passive income, and portfolio income. Passive incomes from business earnings, such as an investment property, restricted organization, or any other business in which an individual doesn't actively participate--such as a quiet financial supporter.

Many people who advocate passive income will be proponents of a work-from-home and work for yourself lifestyle. As of late, passive income is a term that has been used a lot. It's a term that describes money acquired without exertion and is used informally.

When passive income is used as a specialized term it is described by the IRS by the same nominal "Internal Revenue Service", or "income from an enterprise in which the person does not substantially participate," and can sometimes include self-charged interests.

Types of Passive Income

There are two main types of passive income streams: low investment and high investment.

Low investment income streams with low hazards will likely require less money to start and may not be as lucrative. Your earning potential may be limited, and it might take longer to start bringing in the money.

Two of the most popular passive income streams that are low investment includes branch advertising and publishing content to a blog.

High investment income streams require more money at the beginning. While the potential for higher earnings is greater, there's also more risk. Purchase-to-let properties and profit-paying stock are the most lucrative passive income streams for high-income investors.

What Amount Would You Be Able to Earn from Passive Income?

It all depends on the income stream you choose. It might take longer to start earning money with a low investment option, such as publishing content to a blog. Your income will likely be lower.

You can earn more from a high investment income stream like property investment; however, you'll require more funding to begin, and the danger is higher.

It is important to remember that while it isn't normal to earn dynamic income, passive income is unlimited. This is why people find it so interesting.

Some people manage to make ends meet with passive income. However, it is valuable to start earning dynamic income from a traditional job in the beginning stages as there is no guarantee that you will earn enough money to support yourself and your family.

Some types of passive income include self-charged investment properties and income from businesses that the individual receiving income does not participate in. There are explicit IRS decisions that should be continued with the goal for income to be viewed as passive.

Self-Charged Interest

Pass-through products are businesses or companies that have the money credited to them. This means that the interest income from the loan to their portfolio income can be considered passive income. "Certain self-charged interest income or allowances might be treated as passive activity gross income or passive action derivations in case the advance returns are utilized in a passive action," the IRS states.

Investment Properties

Passive income can be characterized with several exceptions when it comes to investment properties. Any rental income that you make as a realtor is considered dynamic income. If you are scrupulous*, it means that you have a property and rent it out to an organization or company where you run a business.* This income doesn't count as passive income unless the rent was approved before 1988. In which case, you can be exempted from having that income classified as passive. The IRS notes, "It doesn't make any difference whether or not the usage is under a rent, and assistance agreement, or some other arrangement."

Nevertheless, income from renting real estate doesn't qualify as passive income. Despite this, a real estate owner can profit from passive income misfortune rules if the property nets a misfortune during the tax year.

Any earnings from real estate you own for investment would be considered dynamic; "No material involvement in a business."

Assuming you put $500,000 into a sweets store with the understanding that the proprietors would pay you a level of earnings, that would be viewed as passive income as long as you don't take part in the activity of the business in any significant manner other than investing.

Many people confuse the concepts of passive income and real estate investing. While passive investing can include real estate, it is not always done in the way that financial backers believe. Passive real estate investment can be one way to make a significant amount of money. Before we get into the specific benefits of passive real estate investment, let's first explain what it is and then, equally important, why dynamic real estate investing is so special.

Many people see renting out private property, such as a single-family home, condo unit, or high-rise, as passive real estate investment. They view this as passive income because, as they envision the investment playing out, they will just purchase a piece of property, lease it out, and afterward gather and take a look at consistently from the inhabitants. However, this isn't a passive real estate contribution.

The financial backer should at least choose the property to purchase and then work with an executive organization to determine normal choices regarding matters such as which occupants to acknowledge and whether to repair or replace a damaged water heater or when to re-floor or paint the property. If the financial backer does not decide to re-appropriate the functional assignments to a property board organization, they must deal with the daily obligations of claiming the actual asset. This is a dynamic real estate contribution.

Assuming you need to earn smart passive income, here are a portion of the primary things you'll have to do:

- Research your options – work out which passive income stream best suits your abilities and conditions.
- Contribute the valuable time and money to get everything rolling – you'll normally have to put away startup money or time before you can begin earning from passive income sources
- Try not to anticipate quick outcomes – most passive income ideas need you to set aside time and effort to begin bringing in money, so you'll have to be patient.
- Keep your normal employment – even though it could be enticing to leave your place of employment, it's ideal to continue earning dynamic income while setting up your passive income streams.
- Increase your income streams - If you have the chance and the money to do so, it may prove beneficial to work at more than one passive income source. This will allow you to earn even if one idea doesn't work.

What Is Passive Real Estate Investing?

Passive real estate investing is a form of real estate investment in which you put your capital into a venture that doesn't require you to make do or your presence.

You can passively put resources into real estate in many ways — for example, by buying stock in real estate-related businesses that are public. These can incorporate real estate improvement organizations, huge real estate agents, or development organizations. You can likewise put resources into Real Estate Investment Trusts (REITs), which are organizations that pool financial backers' funding to put resources into huge real estate bargains.

What's more, thanks to the demand of real estate crowdfunding, you can now likewise make direct investments in individual real estate agreements by pooling your capital with different financial investors in debt-based or equity investments — while still partaking in each of the expected advantages of passive real estate investing.

When you invest in real estate via a crowdfunding platform, you have the option of finding bargains and regularly obligatory investments that can pay you an appropriate, regular installment over a predetermined time. There are also crowdfunding opportunities that allow you to purchase a valuable stake in an arrangement. This will give you the opportunity to share in the ongoing income and the definitive benefits of the property. You can then reap the potential benefits once the income has been distributed.

With a few goals, you can passively invest in real estate. You can, for example, contribute to passive income. This could be in the form of standard profits in a value-based investment or fixed installments (with an interest) in an obligation-based investment. You can also passively invest in real estate development. Overall, you get the appreciation of the properties and the benefit when the assets are traded. Passive real estate investing can also be a viable option to generate both a steady income and long-term development opportunities.

Assuming that you are searching for a passive income stream, real estate can be one of the most mind-blowing passive investment vehicles accessible, given the chances, we will clarify underneath. For the present, what is imperative to comprehend is that passive real estate investing can be an incredible method for adding to your income.

What Is Residual Income?

The income known as residual income refers to income that is determined monthly -- the remaining income for an individual or business after all costs and obligations have been met.

The term residual income is also used in personal finance to refer to income that can be considered discretionary. It is income or salary that remains after an individual pays his mortgage, car loan, and other monthly expenses. Residual income is a key component of personal finances.

How Can You Generate Additional Residual Income?

One way to generate additional residual income is by creating passive-income investments. Your capital is placed in a value-organized or obligation investment, such as stocks, real estate, etc., and you receive a normal income stream. Because you only make one capital investment, the normal installments are added to your income.

Passive real estate investment is a great way to make extra income, as we explained earlier. Here are four reasons passive real estate can be a great way to increase your wealth.

4 Reasons Passive Income Investing Might Be for You

In a value-organized investment, passive real estate permits tax-conceded cash returns that can allow you to keep a greater amount of your earnings.

This is why we have previously stated that real estate can be an impressive passive investment. Real estate ownership has a pass-through potential advantage that allows you to offset your income by taking part in the devaluation cost. This is not the case with stock profits or interest installments.

You Won't Have to Deal with Toilets, Tenants, or Trash

At the point when you are a passive real estate financial backer, you don't manage the problems of everyday management. Leaky faucet? You're not getting a call at 2 am. Broken entrance? It's not your duty to call the jack of all trades.

You Won't Have to Deal with a Bank

It is difficult to work with banks to obtain financing. Banks have become more demanding in obtaining loans since the downturn in the economy. This interaction can be both tedious and depressing.

When you become a passive real-estate financial investor, your investment will be attached to an expert private investment group that has relationships with selected banks. They will explore bank financing options for you so that you don't have to.

Your Passive Investment Lets You Leverage the Expertise and Experience of Others

In general, you have the option to invest in your way. This is true regardless of whether it involves investing through an internet-based financier or buying an investment property. However, it is a great idea to use the knowledge of others.

Passive real estate investing is possible because many real estate financial backers dedicate their lives to learning all about the market.

You Can Make Money While You Sleep

Passive real estate investing can be quick. If you are persistent, do the legal work online and quickly move your reserves. What's more, when your investment is handled, you become a valued partner in that real estate wander and can begin acknowledging passive income as well as a piece of that adventure's development.

You can make money even while you're sleeping. Your money will work for you every day, especially if you invest in properties that have occupants who are earning income.

Chapter 2

Passive income is money you earn that doesn't require you to do a lot of "active" work to continue making it. In essence, you can do most of the work upfront and put some additional effort along the way to earn an income.

For example, if you create an online course, you just need to update its content to keep the money flowing.

You've probably heard the expression, "make money while you sleep." That's the biggest draw that entices people to earn passive income.

You can create something (a blog, course, eBook, videos, or an online store) that generates money even when you're not working. Or you can make passive income investments (property or stocks) that allow you to earn passively.

Myths About Passive Income

1. The **greatest** myth about passive income streams is that it requires no work at all. All income requires work on some level. Except for inheritance, which required the effort of someone from your

generation. It wasn't created by chance. Neither does passive income. To make money, you need to put in some effort. This could include finding the best dividend-paying investment business. Or you could plan a course that you can sell online. After you've done all the work upfront, your product should continue to sell without much of your input.

2. The **second** myth to discredit is that passive income is just a financial buzzword you see on Instagram. Passive income is a very real possibility for everyone. It just takes a bit of creativity to see what you can offer. But passive income is a real thing. You can make some serious money if you put your mind to it, so do try it for yourself.

3. The **third** myth is that passive income is a fast way to make money. Very few passive income ideas generate money instantly. Some of the passive income streams below are faster than others. For example, stock photography has a pretty fast turnaround. You might receive a paycheck in your first month. Building a blog or YouTube channel is

much more work. It could take months or even years for the passive income to start flowing. Be prepared for a delay when you first start a passive income project.

Now that we have discussed in detail passive income and how it could be used effectively to make it a legitimate source of income, let us discuss some ideas that could help you.

Designing and Selling T-Shirts Online Can Be Amazing and Profitable.

Anyone can start an online business. It takes little time to get started.

You can also start your t-shirt company today without investing much capital.

Such opportunities to start an internet-based business from scratch without investment are uncommon. Such countless individuals hop into it without any achievement.

In this way, there is tough competition waiting for you.

These questions might be at the forefront of your mind:

- Does it truly work?
- If yes, how does it work?
- Do I have to print and ship t-shirts?
- How do I start a t-shirt business?

You will find that the right answers are simple and motivating. Continue reading.

You can make a lot of money selling t-shirts online. Some entrepreneurs make $1000 a day selling t-shirts.

Selling t-shirt designs can bring in lots of cash.

You can sell customized t-shirts, you can sell the plans, you can bring in cash with t-shirt affiliate programs.

Running your t-shirt store is an exciting one, but before you get to see the money coming in, you'll need to focus on work a little.

There are some essential steps you'll need to take to start an effective t-shirt business.

- Find your target audience and specialty.

Although you may be the first person in your circle to sell t-shirts online, other merchants have the same goal. Before you start planning and setting up your online store, think about who will buy your t-shirts.

- If your answer is "everybody," you're entering a danger zone.

This will cost you time and money. Who wants that?

You are currently part of the fashion and apparel industry because you have effectively chosen to sell T-shirts.

Although this is a good start, it won't help you to identify your target audience as everyone may not be able to wear t shirts either according to their religion or culture.

To find a product niche, you will need to research your target market (audience) according to their dress style, age, location, sex, and even consider culture.

Hint: Culture and even music plays a significant role in potential customers choosing their t-shirt design for the day or night. For instance, people who listen to rock music or reggae music may dress a little different.

Merch by Amazon

Merch by Amazon is a print-on-demand (POD) service running on Amazon's platform. Print-on-demand service is a process where individuals can create and upload their designs to customize T-shirts, hoodies, hats, etc., and sell them on a pre-order basis, receiving royalty from each sale.

Why is print on demand so attractive? Because it allows you to have an online business at no cost, and it requires little to no time to maintain your business. From the moment you upload your designs, everything after-sale is managed by the POD provider. Printing, packing, shipping is done by the supplier, and you don't have to pay anything.

The first thing you need to do is to sign up for the Merch account. Since Merch by Amazon became an extremely popular POD supplier, Amazon restricted registrations, and now you need to apply for the account before you can start selling.

Now it's time for you to upload your incredible designs. In the beginning, you will be limited to 10 designs max, and you can upload not more than three designs per day. Once you sell 10 T-shirts per month, your tier will go up.

If you don't have designs ready yet, then it's time to start making them. If you are a skilled graphic designer, most likely you will be using Photoshop for your work, and this is excellent software for designing your Tee's as well. Otherwise, you can use Gimp or Canva.

Chapter 3

Passive income through advertising a car

A a lot of people make passive income by promoting their cars. This passive income source can be a good option if you enjoy driving. If you like driving people around, doing tasks for them, and leasing your parking spot for them; then this passive income source is for you. You can make passive income by publicizing your vehicle.

Would you be able to Make Passive Income by Advertising with Your Car? Passive income can be generated by promoting your vehicle. Organizations looking to place versatile ads on it can "lease" its publicizing space. You are providing sponsors with a place to display their ads, and you get a commission or passive income monthly.

It's a mutually beneficial arrangement for promoting organizations and anybody with a vehicle. These organizations don't need to get their vehicles and drive them around. Also, you get to bring in cash without making any investments or get some much-needed rest from your everyday employment. Sounds simple, isn't that so?

You may be cruising in your car, but that doesn't necessarily mean you are ready for publicizing. You have some requirements that you need to meet. Every organization has its own set of requirements. However, the following are some basic guidelines. You ought to:

- Be of legal driving age
- Be a functioning driver
- Have a vehicle
- Have cutting-edge full collision protection and a decent driving history record.

Depending upon the company you pick, you will most likely need consent to save the advertisement on your vehicle for the whole agreement length. These organizations may likewise require a certain amount of mileage you need to drive every week/month. You may find yourself driving in areas with high traffic (both pedestrian and auto) from time to time.

Chapter 4

Affiliate Marketing

Affiliate marketing helps different brands or organizations sell their products or services, and on the other hand, you're helping customers track down the best product and service for them.

You could make a profit by promoting products through blog posts and digital recordings. You earn a commission when people buy products using the affiliate interface that you provided.

Affiliate marketers can sell the product or service of another entity and earn a commission for each deal they make. Affiliate promoting, if done well, can provide a steady stream of passive income. Many blogs promote affiliate marketing as a quick way to make a lot of money which is far from reality.

Affiliate promoting is challenging work that needs commitment and dedication. There is so much to do, from finding the right products to maintaining blogs, it can be exhausting but quite lucrative as well.

The affiliate program you choose to promote is a major factor in your ability to earn benefits as an affiliate. No matter if you are looking for something once or repeatedly, your ability to showcase success as an affiliate depends entirely on the program's income planning need and how much you're willing to invest in these programs.

- One Commission Model
- Repeating Commission Model.

This is a very simple model. You will get more referrals, which means you can obtain a higher commission. To get your bonus, you will need to promote a product to potential customers via an internet-based medium. This is because affiliate showcasing programs use a reference URL interface. You make a commission when a client plans to purchase a product.

Chapter 5

Sell Digital Files on Etsy

This new world of informational and downloadable products is exploding right now, and Etsy is a great hub to sell and deliver them. A digital product is anything that is delivered electronically (digital files) rather than physically (packaged and shipped). This could include printable worksheets or forms, vector illustrations, and digital patterns, fonts, e-books or step-by-step guides, stock photography, design templates, sewing patterns, printable art, or signage, or even logos and icons.

Setting up a digital listing is the same as setting up a physical listing, with a few exceptions. You'll start by clicking Add a Listing under Listings Manager. When you create your listing, you'll select "Digital" as the listing type (seventh option under Listing Details). You can also select your listing to renew automatically under Renewal Options (sixth option under Listing Details). To go with your listing, you'll need to include clear imagery to show your product.

It's also important to include some disclaimer information in each digital listing's description about what customers are allowed to do with their products, how colors are viewed on-screen vs. print, and how you handle refunds since the product is delivered immediately. It's also good to put all this info in your Shop Policies as well.

After the description, the next section is called Digital Files. Here you can upload up to 5 different files – if your product has more than 5 files, you can also upload a zipped file (which counts as one file). There's also a button in this section that allows you to add a special note to buyers of your digital purchases.

The last section to fill out as you prep your listing is the Search Terms. Some popular general terms to include here for digital products (as long as they accurately represent your product) would be digital, download, instant download, printable, and PDF (or whatever file type it is).

Chapter 6

Rent out your car

If you haven't been driving much recently, you might be contemplating how much your car is costing you as it sits in your carport. Fortunately, you can bring in cash leasing your car, similarly as you would leasing your home on Airbnb or a comparative stage. This is what you want to know.

There are a few car-sharing companies through which you can lease your car when you're not utilizing it.

1. **Avail a Car Sharing**

Profit rents cars at airport terminals across the country. They are available to voyaging individuals who would like to leave their car at an air terminal for the duration of their trip. You drop your car off at the air terminal and they show it on their application. When someone needs your car, they will get it at the terminal and then return it when they are done.

Profit shows you that you can lease your car for as little as $25 per day and that the average income for a four-day rental of your car is $80. Profit Plus is only for people who plan to rent the car for at least a month or more. Avail Plus will reward you with $400 if you list your car for thirty consecutive days. This is regardless of how long it has been leased.

2. **HyreCar**

HyreCar is a leader in the leasing of cars to individuals who use them for Lyft, Uber, or other conveyance services. You can lease on a daily, weekly, or monthly basis.

Keep in mind that some Uber and Lyft drivers can drive a lot of miles with their cars. If you lease through HyreCar you should expect to see your mileage rise quickly.

Chapter 7

Udemy

If you are looking for a new friendly way to grow a passive income online then learning how to make money with Udemy or one of the growing bands of Online Course Marketplaces is a great place to start.

You don't need to buy a domain, set up hosting, create Clickbank accounts, upload videos to Amazon S3, and do all the other tasks associated with setting up an online business. Many skilled Internet Marketers are repurposing their content on sites like Udemy. Content stretching is taking one piece and spreading it to as many markets and media outlets as possible.

What Do You Need to Get Started?

All you need to get started are these few items…

1) Computer/Laptop

2) A decent microphone

3) Screen recording software

To achieve success on Udemy, you don't have to be already an "expert" in your field. You probably already know a lot more about a certain topic than most people. You don't have to be afraid of being on camera, or if your voice isn't what you want, you can just get over that fear. Do not be afraid to take action if you aren't considered "expert enough" to sell your products. You can use your credentials in places such as your profile or bio on these platforms if you have impressive credentials. If you don't have any, it's okay. Just be honest. Be creative and show off your strengths and achievements. Your profile is your chance to shine and brag about them.

Chapter 8

Create an app

Mobile apps can turn individuals into overnight millionaires if they hit it right. Remember Angry Birds? Even if you can't be as successful as Angry Bird, you can still earn some passive income every month for the next 5–10 years via a mobile app. The best part of it all, once you publish the app, you will be generating passive income for the next few years until people stop using mobile app technology.

This guide is for those who don't know how to make passive income from mobile apps. How do you publish your app? This is the function of your Google Developer Account. You will use it for publishing apps to Google Play Store.

For a one-time registration, you will need to spend $25. It's then all free. It takes only a few minutes to create apps and publish them. Now you're done with all the account registration. Now, it's time for you to create your app.

This step will consume most of your time. However, unless you hire someone to build the app, no money is required.

You should have an idea of the app you want. People will download any app that solves their problems. For example, public holiday calendar app, alarm clock app, education app, and so on. You don't need to build a mega app such as WhatsApp or Twitter. You might be wrong if you believe you are unable to create an app due to your lack of programming knowledge.

Chapter 9

Create a blog or YouTube channel

You give YouTube your consent that they can run ads before, during, or after your videos. You get to choose what type of ad placements you're comfortable with, press a few buttons, and Google does the rest.

Once set up, Google will show ads on your videos, and every time someone sees (or clicks) on those ads, both you and YouTube split the fee that Google charges the advertiser. The split is 45% for YouTube and 55% for the creator. It's safe to say that to get any views on YouTube, you're going to need a channel to start. YouTube walks you through how to do it on this page, the next step to any YouTube channel is to create content that your audience will love. It is best to focus on a particular niche and dive into the content that they'll enjoy.

YouTube was open to any channel to join its program immediately after it started. However, abusers began to abuse the system so YouTube had to modify the rules to ensure that channels were legitimate.

After you have met all the eligibility requirements, then you can apply for an AdSense Account. This is how you will make money with ads. Take your time and answer all questions correctly. There are many ways to make money with your YouTube channel once you have been accepted into the YouTube Partner Program.

- **Ad Revenue:** To begin making ad revenue, you need to turn on ads within YouTube. Doing so will make it so the ads will play when people see your videos, which will lead to you getting paid. Pay attention to your CPM metrics here, this is crucial to know how much you can make with more views.

- **YouTube Red (Premium) Revenue:** Every time that a YouTube premium account watches your videos, you'll get a small portion of their subscription fee. This isn't a ton of extra money, but it also doesn't take any extra effort on your behalf to make it happen.

- **Channel Memberships:** Once your channel has over 1,000 subscribers, you can set up channel memberships for your subscribers. This allows you to charge a fee every month for them to see some of your exclusive content and you can even offer other perks for members of different tiered levels.

- **Launch Your Merchandise Shelf:** Once you have over 10,000 subscribers, you're eligible to launch a merchandise shelf on your channel. This allows you to sell merchandise directly on your channel below your videos. This is great if you have a saying or catch-phrase that resonates with your following.

- **Super Chat and Super Sticker:** These interactive elements allow users to pay to be seen in your live streams by purchasing a "super chat" or "super sticker" so that you see them.

Chapter 10

Rent out different items

Taking advantage of the things you already have can be a great way to make money. While there are plenty of different side hustle ideas you can pursue, one of the fastest ways to make money is to sell your stuff.

Another way to make money from your stuff is by renting it out to others. Renting your possessions isn't just a way to make some quick money. It can also become a regular side hustle that turns your things into income-generating assets. Best of all, it can be a side hustle that doesn't take much of your time to maintain.

When you're renting things out, you'll be making money by leveraging assets you already have (passive income), not by working more hours. You may need to put a little bit of time into the side hustle, but it's not like you're trading time for money. This can be a great fit if you have a tight schedule and limited extra time for more work.

Many people need a specific tool but don't want to buy it because they may not need it again in the future. If you own the tools, you can rent them as a way to make money. This applies to all types of tools, from saws to drywall lifts to chainsaws. Lawn and landscaping equipment like mowers and leaf blowers are also good options. Most towns and cities have equipment rental businesses, but you could also start doing this on a small scale.

Some sites allow you to rent out about anything. If you have something that you want to rent out, but you're not sure where to list it, these general rental sites may be a great option:

- **Fat Llama** – One of the most popular websites for renting just about anything. The site claims that average lenders make $50 per week and top lenders make up to $3,000 per month.

- **Loanables** – Another general rental site where you can list things like appliances, musical instruments, furniture, and more.

- **Rentah** – List things like party supplies, tools, sporting goods, outdoor items, fashion, electronics, and more. You can also list some services like childcare and entertainment.

Falling into the same category, you can also make good money by renting out your wedding dress. There are a lot of brides looking to save money on a wedding dress, and renting one is a wonderful way to do it. If you're not overly sentimental about your wedding dress, this could be a great option.

Chapter 11

Sell Stock Photos

If you're a photographer looking to make a bit more money, you've probably been tempted, at least at some point, to go into stock photography.

Perhaps you had hoped to find a way to sell the many unused photos on your hard drives. Perhaps you were interested in having your photos sold by someone else.

Stock photography simply refers to generic imagery that is used by buyers for visual content on news stories, blogs, and websites. It can also be used to design material for ads or promotional materials.

It's much cheaper than hiring a photographer and is generally sold through a platform that specializes in keeping a large library full of such images so that buyers have several different options to choose from.

Think of stock photography as the opposite of custom-made photographs, which are licensed directly to a client (depending on copyright status) and are original works created specifically for that client's purpose.

Chapter 12

Become a Drop-shipper

Drop shipping can be a passive income source. This is done by choosing the market and niche you want to target, conducting market research, finding a supplier, building an online store, and creating a marketing strategy to drive targeted traffic. You can either sell items you don't own or things you have. These are the two options available to you. You can either sell physical or digital products.

You'll need to find a company that is willing to dropship directly to your customer and you'll want to make sure your wholesale company has a good reputation. If they ship items too slowly, or products run out of stock often, you're going to look bad to customers who think you're filling their orders.

Conduct an online search of wholesale companies that sell the products you want to offer. Be on the lookout for people who claim to be a wholesaler but aren't wholesale companies. A legitimate wholesaler will usually require an application and won't charge you sales tax.

There are many free shopping carts out there and those may work well if you only sell a few products. But, if you plan to have a lot of inventory, or you want to offer promotional codes, you'll need a more sophisticated cart. Fees vary greatly, so you'll want to do some research to determine which cart will work best with your e-commerce site.

Consider selling products on other websites, like eBay or Amazon. It's important to test your wholesaler out first to ensure that they're able to deliver reputable products on time. Otherwise, bad reviews could tarnish your reputation and get you banned from selling in those marketplaces.

Chapter 13

Refinancing your mortgage

Whether you need additional funds for an upcoming large purchase, take money out to invest in real estate, or just want to get a better interest rate for your home loan, one option you can consider is refinancing. Cash-out refinances will replace the existing mortgage with another loan that has a higher balance.

Sometimes the terms of the new loan are more favorable than those of the existing loan. The homeowner gets the difference in cash A cash-out refinance is an excellent way for you to borrow money and refinance your mortgage simultaneously. Your mortgage will be refinanced, and you will get a check during closing.

The balance that you will owe on the new mortgage is going to be higher than that of your old one. It will be based on the amount of the check and other closing costs added to the loan. The result is that you will increase the mortgage principle that you owe PLUS you will have extra money given to you at the close of the mortgage process.

There are no restrictions when it comes to using the proceeds you get from the cash-out refinance. This means that you can use it for whatever you need but expect that there will still be tax consequences. Cash-out refinances works like the combination of a home equity loan and refinancing. You will be able to borrow the cash you need, just like with a line of credit or home equity loan.

There are several common reasons for you to choose a cash-out to refinance.

Below are some of the scenarios when you might want to consider a cash-out refinance:

- You want to use the money to invest it into another property to make more money in passive income each month.
- You want to use the equity on your home to pay for some improvements that can increase the overall value of your property.
- You encountered some unexpected expenses like expensive and urgent car repairs or emergency medical bills.

- You want to pay off the high balance or high-interest credit cards or get rid of other high-interest debts to save money.
- You need some help to pay for the college education of your child or children.

You want to make the most out of the possible benefit of tax deduction concerning the interest paid on the mortgage loan. Just remember that even if you might be in any of the situations above, it is important to think about your decision first to determine if a cash-out refinance is the most sensible option for you.

Chapter 14

Car Wash

If you don't want to be an employee for your entire life, and you find that office hours from 9 a.m. to 5 p.m. just do not suit your needs, you might consider creating a passive income. It is characterized by the fact that you first invest your time or money. The result is that you eventually make a profit.

There are different options.

There are multiple ways of building a passive income. A popular example is an author who spends time and effort on his book and then enjoys the royalties. This works very well in a few cases, but in many cases not at all. Another option would be to speculate with stocks and shares. However, this requires certain skills and exceptional knowledge of the money market. In addition, there is a remarkably elevated risk of making high losses. Somewhat more secure alternatives are investments in property that you can rent, or in automatically operated service equipment such as car washes. Even self-service car washes are not fully autonomous.

Having a self-service car wash does not mean you do not have to worry about it at all. As users put coins in the machine, you don't have to be there. However, the washing chemicals need to be replenished periodically and money should be taken out frequently. You should also make sure that your system is functioning properly and get it serviced at the right times. Mark VII has a network of service providers that can quickly reach you to fix your site. For repairs, the same is true. The number must be visible so users can report any defects. You can also be reached via this number. This is the only way to respond quickly enough and avoid prolonged downtime or loss of customers.

It also links you to the self-service car wash. Nevertheless, the tasks are less demanding than those in wage-paying jobs. You can therefore plan to spend most of your time somewhere else, whether it's for work, hobbies, or for friends and family.

Chapter 15

Peer-to-peer income

P2P lending directly connects people with idle money lenders; who are interested in lending to people in need of credit, thereby removing intermediary margins. This enables the lenders to earn higher returns from their investments and borrowers to access quick loans at a lower cost.

Lenders receive back the money they lend in the form of EMIs – equated monthly investments – which include both principal and the interest income earned. Every month the borrower repays the lenders through EMIs. The P2P lending platform collects the EMIs on behalf of the lender from the borrower and adds them to the lender's escrow account from where the lender can choose to withdraw or invest again.

Most lenders can earn high and stable returns by building a diversified portfolio. However, building a portfolio that mitigates the risk of default by spreading investment across many borrowers with different risk profiles, demographics, occupations, and others can be time-consuming. P2P lending platforms involve innovative products and processes to cut down on the time and effort needed to build a portfolio.

Conclusion

Some of the most profitable options for generating income include creating an app, investing in real estate or stocks, starting a business that you can run from home, and leasing out property or a car through an app. Of course, it's always best to do your research and find the option that best suits your interests and skill set.

Passive income is never *really passive.*

To achieve financial independence, many people set up passive income sources to supplement their full-time jobs or replace them. Individuals of all backgrounds can build wealth by generating passive income. This allows them to spend more time on hobbies, socializing with friends and relaxing.

While passive income is often portrayed as easy money, it's hard work. This includes building an audience, optimizing paid advertisements, and providing a wonderful customer experience. However, as a current or aspiring business owner, you're not afraid to put in the time to do all of those things, and you might already have all three checked off your list.

Passive income streams can be added to an existing business to create a new revenue source that has a different economic basis. These income streams are more likely to have higher profit margins than physical products and scale faster, giving you greater flexibility in your business.

If you are just starting, a high profit-margin product is a great way for you to grow your business and make money to invest in the next phase. However, you must be aware that it will require work, even though it is called passive income.

Passive income can be a great way to keep cash flow to the bank as you sleep. While it sounds efficient, it's important to remember that it still requires work, time, and sometimes money upfront. No income stream is completely passive and there are a lot of diverse ways to go about making money through this method. As long as you know your audience, give them what they want, and persist, you will see the funds roll in.

Finally, always remember PERSISTENCE is key. DO NOT GIVE UP! Try new ideas and keep going until you succeed!

Made in the USA
Monee, IL
04 November 2026

67376098R00036